EXCELLENT SCIENCE EXPERIMENTS

EXPERIMENTS WITH ELECTRICITY and MAGNETS

Chris Oxlade
Consultant: John Farndon

PowerKids press

Published in 2015 by **The Rosen Publishing Group, Inc.**
29 East 21st Street, New York, NY 10010

Library of Congress Cataloging-in-Publication Data

Oxlade, Chris.
Experiments with electricity and magnets / by Chris Oxlade.
p. cm. — (Excellent science experiments)
Includes index.
ISBN 978-1-4777-5962-2 (pbk.)
ISBN 978-1-4777-5963-9 (6-pack)
ISBN 978-1-4777-5804-5 (library binding)
1. Electricity — Experiments — Juvenile literature. 2. Magnetism —
Experiments — Juvenile literature. I. Oxlade, Chris. II. Title.
QC527.2 O95 2015
537.078—d23

© 2015 Miles Kelly Publishing

Publishing Director: Belinda Gallagher
Creative Director: Jo Cowan
Editors: Amanda Askew, Claire Philip
Editorial Assistant: Lauren White
Designers: Joe Jones, Kayleigh Allen
Cover Designer: Simon Lee

Photographer: Alex Bibby
Production Manager: Elizabeth Collins
Reprographics: Stephan Davis, Thom Allaway,
Anthony Cambray, Jennifer Hunt,
Lorraine King

ACKNOWLEDGEMENTS
The publishers would like to thank the following sources for the use of their photographs:
Shutterstock.com Cover Ohn Mar; 6 sydeen; 7 Nir Levy; 11(c) Yobidaba, (bl) koya979, (br)
Elena Elisseeva. Every effort has been made to acknowledge the source and copyright holder
of each picture. Miles Kelly Publishing apologies for any unintentional errors or omissions.

Printed in the United States of America
CPSIA Compliance Information: Batch CW15PK: For Further Information contact Rosen Publishing, New York, New York at 1-800-237-9932

CONTENTS

Learn lots about electricity and how it works!

Experiment time!

How can you light two bulbs? Find out on page 15.

Help needed

Help and hazards

• All of the experiments are suitable for young readers to conduct, but you will need help and supervision with some. This is usually because the experiment requires the use of sharp equipment. These experiments are marked with a "Help needed" symbol.

• Read the instructions together with an adult before starting, and have an adult help to assemble the equipment and supervise the experiment.

• It may be useful for an adult to do a risk assessment to avoid any possible hazards before you begin. Check that long hair and any loose clothing are tied back.

• Be careful when handling wire strippers, scissors, or knives, and ensure that wires and nails are put away safely after use.

What is ELECTRICITY?

Electricity is a kind of energy, and a major source of power for much of the world. It powers many of the machines we use every day. Electricity is produced in power stations, either by burning coal, oil, or gas, or by using water or nuclear reactors to turn huge turbines.

Creating a flow

Electricity as a power source depends on electrons, which are tiny parts of atoms. When electrons are pushed, they hop from one atom to the next. When billions of electrons are pushed, electricity flows. The push comes from a battery or a power station.

Electric wire

Atom

Moving electron

Materials

Conductors are substances through which electricity can flow. Metals such as copper conduct electricity well.

Insulators are materials, such as wood and plastic, that do not allow electricity to flow.

Electric circuits

An electric circuit is an unbroken loop of conducting material, along which electricity can flow. The three basic parts of an electric circuit are – an energy source such as a battery, a conductor, and an object for the circuit to power, such as a lightbulb.

An electric current flows through the copper conductor on the inside of the wire.

The outer covering is made of a plastic insulator, to stop electricity from escaping.

Lightbulb

Conductor

Battery

4

Electricity in ACTION

Electricity is always at work around us – even when we can't see it! This is because all atoms can become electrically charged. Usually the balance between an atom's negatively charged electrons and positively charged center is equal, but if the electrons are lost by being "pushed," the object becomes positively charged. If electrons are gained, the object becomes negatively charged.

Static electricity

This is the buildup of electric charge on a surface. When you rub two materials together, electrons move from one object to the other – leaving one object positively charged and one negatively charged.

After a balloon is rubbed on hair, the hair stands up! Each strand has become positively charged, so they repel and move apart.

Attract or repel

Objects with opposite charges attract each other, and charges that are the same push each other apart (repel).

A negative charge from the cloud meets a positive charge from the ground.

Lightning spark

A lightning bolt is a dramatic display of natural electricity. During a thunderstorm, a negative electrical charge builds up at the base of a cloud, while the ground has a positive charge. A lightning spark jumps between them to release the charge.

Magnetic force

Electricity is closely linked with magnetism – the invisible force between magnetic materials. When electricity moves, magnetism is created, and when magnets move, electricity is created. Magnets are pieces of metal that can attract magnetic materials, such as iron.

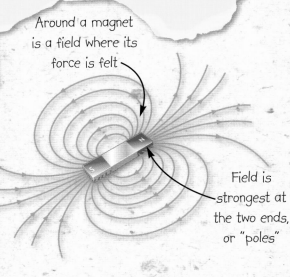

Around a magnet is a field where its force is felt

Field is strongest at the two ends, or "poles"

Using this book

Each experiment has numbered instructions and clear explanations about your findings. Read through all the instructions before you start an experiment, and then follow them carefully, one at a time. If you are not sure what to do, ask an adult.

Experiment symbols

① Shows how long the experiment will take once you have collected all the equipment you need.

② Shows if you need to ask an adult to help you with the experiment.

③ Shows how easy or difficult the experiment is to do.

Introduction
See what you will be learning about in each experiment.

Things you will need
You should be able to find the equipment around the house, from a supermarket, or from a hardware store. No special equipment is needed. Always ask before using materials from home.

⚠ Safety
If there is a "Help needed" symbol at the start of the experiment, you must ask an adult to help you.

The warning symbol also tells you to be careful when using knives or scissors. Always ask an adult for help.

ELECTRIC balloons

Does your hair sometimes stand on end when you brush or comb it? This is static electricity at work. When different materials rub against each other, electricity jumps from one material to the other.

①	②	③
30 min	Help needed	Easy

You will need
- work surface
- 3 balloons
- wool (sock or glove)
- small scraps of paper (such as tissue paper)
- metal spoon
- cotton thread, 3 ft.
- water
- scissors

1a Blow up a balloon and tie a knot in its neck. Rub the balloon with wool, such as a glove or sock.

1b Cut the paper into small squares

Move the balloon over the small scraps of paper and watch what happens.

Also try...
Put a charged balloon next to your hair, or near a trickle of water from a tap, and watch what happens.

Q Can a balloon pick up paper?

A Yes, when it has static electricity on its surface. Rubbing the balloon with wool creates a collection of electricity, called static electricity, on the surface. Tiny particles called electrons move from the wool to the balloon, giving the balloon a negative charge. This negative charge attracts positive electric charges in the paper. As the pieces of paper are small, the pull is big enough to pick them up.

10

Also try...
Simple mini-experiments to test the science you've learned.

Doing the experiments

✴ Clear a surface to work on, such as a table, and cover it with newspaper if you need to.

✴ You could wear an apron or an old t-shirt to protect your clothing.

✴ Gather all the equipment you need before you start, and tidy up after each experiment.

✴ Ask an adult to help you when an experiment is marked with a "Help needed" or warning symbol.

✴ Work over a tray or sink when you are pouring water.

✴ Always ask an adult to help if you are unsure what to do.

2a

Wet a metal spoon and rub it all over the surface of the balloon.

Blow up two more balloons. Tie the end of the cotton thread to the neck of one of them, then rub both balloons all over with wool.

2b

Now test the effect of this by moving the balloon over the pieces of paper again. What happens this time?

3b

Don't let the balloons touch each other

Ask a helper to hold the top of the length of thread, letting the balloon hang down. Move the other balloon towards it. Watch what happens to the hanging balloon.

Q Can you get rid of static electricity?

A Yes, rubbing the balloon with a wet spoon removes its charge. The static electricity on the balloon's surface flows away into the spoon (the water helps this happen by improving the metal's contact with the balloon). Now the balloon has no charge, so it can no longer attract the bits of paper.

Labels
Handy labels will provide you with useful tips and information to help your experiment run smoothly.

Q Can balloons push each other?

A Yes, static electricity pushes the balloons apart. Rubbing the two balloons with wool creates static electricity on the surfaces of the balloons. The charges on both are negative. Charges that are the same (two positive or two negative) always push each other away (repel), so the balloons are pushed apart.

Explanation
At the end of each experiment is a question-and-answer explanation. It tells you what should have happened and why.

Scientist KIT

Before you begin experimenting you will need to gather some equipment. You should be able to find all of it around the house, from a local supermarket or from a hardware store. Ask an adult's permission before using anything and take care when you see a warning sign.

Electrical bits

- 1.5V AA battery
- 1.5V flashlight bulbs (not LED bulbs)
- copper wire
- thin, insulated electrical wire
- wire strippers (or pliers)

Battery

⚠ Warning!

Although it is very useful in everyday life, electricity can be dangerous. It can give off shocks and is particularly dangerous when near water.

Copper wire

Glove

From the Kitchen

- aluminum foil
- aluminum soda can (empty)
- dish towel
- glass
- glass jar
- jug
- knife
- paper towels
- plastic tray
- scissors
- sieve
- spoons (metal)
- table salt
- water

Aluminum foil

From the craft box

- adhesive tape
- cotton thread
- pen
- small scraps of paper, such as tissue paper
- wool (sock or glove)

Scissors

Tissue paper

⚠ Warning!

Scissors and knives are extremely sharp and can cut you easily. Make sure you ask an adult for help. When passing scissors or a knife, always point the handle towards the other person.

Handy hint!

You can get small scraps of paper from a hole punch. They will be all the same shape, and you will be reusing otherwise unwanted paper!

Other stuff

- balloons
- bar magnet
- clothespin
- compass
- copper coin
- large steel nail (or screw)
- masking tape or plastic insulating tape
- paper clips
- plastic document folder

- short, thick elastic band
- talcum powder
- various objects made from different materials, such as paper, wood, glass, plastic, metal
- zinc-coated (galvanized) nail

Clothespin

Balloon

Handy hint!
You could draw silly faces on the balloons using a felt-tip pen. Make sure you wait for the ink to dry before rubbing the balloon with wool.

Copper coins

Places you'll need to work
- work surface

Electrical wire

Remember to recycle and reuse

One way to help the environment is by recycling and reusing materials such as glass, paper, plastics, and scrap metals. It is mostly cheaper and less wasteful than making new products from scratch.

Reusing means you use materials again in their original form rather than throwing them away.

Recycling is when materials are taken to a plant where they can be melted and remade into either the same or new products.

Handy hint!
Most soda cans are made of aluminum and can be recycled. Many supermarkets now have recycling points where you can dispose of your empty cans.

9

ELECTRIC
balloons

Does your hair sometimes stand on end when you brush or comb it? This is static electricity at work. When different materials rub against each other, electricity jumps from one material to the other.

30 min   Help needed   Easy

You will need

- work surface
- 3 balloons
- wool (sock or glove)
- small scraps of paper (such as tissue paper)
- metal spoon
- cotton thread, 3 ft.
- water
- scissors

1a

Blow up a balloon and tie a knot in its neck. Rub the balloon with wool, such as a glove or sock.

1b

Cut the paper into small squares

Move the balloon over the small scraps of paper and watch what happens.

Also try...

Put a charged balloon next to your hair, or near a trickle of water from a tap, and watch what happens.

ⓠ Can a balloon pick up paper?

ⓐ **Yes, when it has static electricity on its surface.** Rubbing the balloon with wool creates a collection of electricity, called static electricity, on the surface. Tiny particles called electrons move from the wool to the balloon, giving the balloon a negative charge. This negative charge attracts positive electric charges in the paper. As the pieces of paper are small, the pull is big enough to pick them up.

Wet a metal spoon and rub it all over the surface of the balloon.

Now test the effect of this by moving the balloon over the pieces of paper again. What happens this time?

ⓠ Can you get rid of static electricity?

ⓐ **Yes, rubbing the balloon with a wet spoon removes its charge.** The static electricity on the balloon's surface flows away into the spoon (the water helps this happen by improving the metal's contact with the balloon). Now the balloon has no charge, so it can no longer attract the bits of paper.

Blow up two more balloons. Tie the end of the cotton thread to the neck of one of them, then rub both balloons all over with wool.

Don't let the balloons touch each other

Ask a helper to hold the top of the length of thread, letting the balloon hang down. Move the other balloon towards it. Watch what happens to the hanging balloon.

ⓠ Can balloons push each other?

ⓐ **Yes, static electricity pushes the balloons apart.** Rubbing the two balloons with wool creates static electricity on the surfaces of the balloons. The charges on both are negative. Charges that are the same (two positive or two negative) always push each other away (repel), so the balloons are pushed apart.

STATIC
patterns

Some photocopiers and computer printers use static electricity to work. The static makes the marks you see on the finished page. Get ready to find out how this process works.

30 min   No help needed   Easy

You will need

- work surface
- plastic document folder
- talcum powder
- sieve
- masking tape or plastic insulating tape
- plastic tray
- paper towels
- water
- scissors

(a)

Shake some talcum powder through a sieve onto a plastic tray. The sieve helps to spread the talcum powder more evenly.

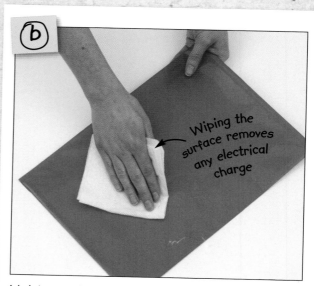

(b)

Wiping the surface removes any electrical charge

Moisten a piece of paper towel with water and wipe it over both sides of your plastic document folder. Then, dry the plastic thoroughly with a piece of paper towel. This will remove any static electricity from the surface of the plastic.

Cut pieces of tape and stick them onto the plastic to make a shape, such as a checkmark. Press the tape down firmly onto the plastic, but fold over the end to make it easy to rip off.

Turn the plastic over, but don't put it down. Very carefully hold it over the tray and lower it slowly, until it is just above the talcum powder.

Now you are ready to make your pattern. Put the plastic on a table and quickly rip off the pieces of tape.

Turn the plastic over to see what's happened.

Q Can I make a shape in talcum powder?

A Yes, using static electricity. Ripping the tape quickly off the plastic document folder creates static electricity where the tape was stuck down. This happens because the tape and plastic are made from different materials. The electric charge attracts the tiny particles of talcum powder to the plastic, making your shape.

Simple electric CIRCUITS

A flashlight makes light using electricity. How does it work? This experiment shows how electricity flows around a loop to make the bulb light up.

15 min   No help needed   Easy

You will need

- work surface
- 1.5V AA battery
- short, thick elastic band
- scissors
- 3 lengths of aluminum foil, 8 in. x 1 in.
- 2 1.5V flashlight bulbs (not LED bulbs)

Preparation: Make a circuit

(a) Fold each of the pieces of foil in half twice, lengthwise, to make thin strips of foil.

Put the small elastic band lengthwise around the battery so that it goes over both metal terminals of the battery.

(b)

(c) Put one end of each foil strip under the elastic band at each end of the battery. Make sure the two strips do not touch each other; otherwise an electric current will flow.

(d)

A flashlight bulb has two terminals (contacts). One is the metal casing below the base of the glass (the screw thread or bayonet prongs); the other is on the bottom. Wrap the end of one of the foil strips around the metal casing and twist it to make it stay in place. Make sure the strip does not touch the contact at the bottom of the bulb.

①

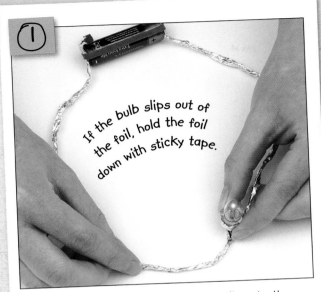

If the bulb slips out of the foil, hold the foil down with sticky tape.

Press the bottom contact of your bulb onto the other foil strip.

②ⓐ

Wrap the second piece of foil around the metal casing of the second bulb.

②ⓑ

Place the third piece of foil on your work surface.

②ⓒ

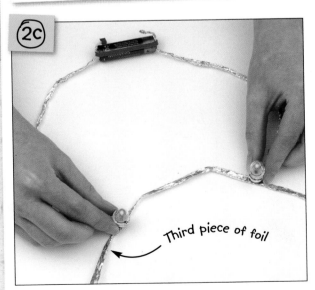

Third piece of foil

Put the bottom contacts of each bulb (which are connected to the battery with foil strips) onto the third piece of foil. What happens?

Ⓠ How does a battery light a bulb?

Ⓐ By connecting the *bulb* to the battery with the foil strips, you make a loop called a **circuit.** Electricity flows around the circuit. This flow is called an electric current. The battery is like a pump that pushes the current around the circuit. The current comes out of the terminal marked + (positive) and goes into the terminal marked − (negative). As the current goes through the *bulb*, it glows.

③

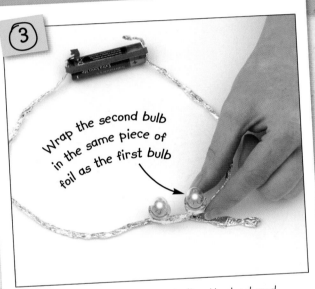

Wrap the second bulb in the same piece of foil as the first bulb

Take the foil strip with the bulb attached and wrap it around the side contact of the second bulb, further down. Press the bottom contacts of the bulbs against the other strip.

Ⓠ Can you make the two bulbs glow brighter?

Ⓐ Yes, by sending the electricity through both bulbs at the same time, not one after the other. We say that the bulbs are connected in "parallel."

Ⓠ How can you light two bulbs?

Ⓐ By putting the bulbs in "series." The electricity flows from the battery, through one bulb, then through the other bulb, and back to the battery. The light from the bulbs is quite dim.

CONDUCTORS
and insulators

Some materials let electricity pass through them easily. Others don't let electricity pass through them at all. Here's an experiment to find out which materials are which.

Preparation: Make a circuit

Page 14 shows how to make your basic circuit. You'll only need two lengths of foil.

You will need

- 1.5V AA battery
- short, thick elastic band
- 1.5V flashlight bulb (not LED bulb)
- 2 lengths of aluminum foil, 8 in. × 1 in.
- scissors
- paper
- pen
- objects made from various materials, such as paper, wood, glass, plastic, metal

(a)

Touch the base of the bulb and the end of the second foil strip on either end of a plastic ruler or pen. What happens to the bulb?

b Repeat step a using other objects. Each time, write down the name of the object and its material in a results table. Put an X next to it if the bulb does not light up, and a check if it does.

OBJECT	MATERIAL	X ✓
Pen	Plastic	X
Ruler	Plastic	
Paper clip	Metal	
Book	Paper	
Pencil	Wood	

key

Metal spoon

Paper clip

Q Which materials let electricity flow through them?

A Metals let electricity flow through them, lighting up the bulb. Metals are conductors. Other materials, including paper, wood, and plastic, don't let electricity flow through them. They are insulators.

DETECTING electricity

30 min   Help needed   Tricky

How can we tell if electricity is flowing along a wire? You need a detector, such as a compass. A compass needle moves when it is near a wire with electricity flowing through it.

You will need

- 1.5V AA battery
- short, thick elastic band
- thin insulated electrical wire, 3 ft.
- 1.5V flashlight bulb (not LED bulb)
- sticky tack
- scissors
- 2 lengths of aluminum foil, 8 in. × 1 in.
- adhesive tape
- wire strippers or a knife
- compass

Preparation: Make a circuit

Page 14 shows how to make your basic circuit. You'll only need two lengths of foil.

Now remove the *bulb* to turn the light off. What happens to the compass needle?

Put the compass on top of one of the foil strips, then touch the strip with the bottom contact of the bulb. This completes the circuit and makes the bulb light up.

Q Can you detect current?

A Yes, the compass needle detects the current. When electricity flows along the foil, it turns the foil into a weak magnet. This makes the compass needle, which is also a magnet, twitch.

Preparation: Strip some wire

Ask an adult to strip 1 inch of insulation from either end of the insulated electrical wire. This can be done with wire strippers or a sharp knife.

Preparation: Make a current detector

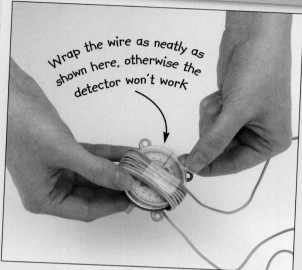

Wrap the wire as neatly as shown here, otherwise the detector won't work

Starting about 8 inches from one end of the wire, wrap the wire around your compass. Finish winding it about 8 inches from the other end. Use adhesive tape and sticky tack to keep the wire in place.

Q Can I make the detector more sensitive?

A **Yes, by wrapping wire around the compass.** This turns the compass into a much stronger magnet when the circuit is complete and electricity is flowing through the wire. The stronger magnet makes the compass needle more sensitive to the flow of electricity.

②

Attach one bare wire end to one of the foil strips, and the other end to the bottom contact of the bulb. Electricity will flow through the wire. Is the compass needle moving differently now?

Battery POWER

All sorts of electric gadgets need a battery to work. A battery is a source of electricity. Batteries make electricity from chemicals. In this experiment, you can see how this happens.

30 min	Help needed	Tricky

You will need

- copper coin or copper wire
- zinc-coated (galvanized) nail or screw
- table salt
- glass
- clothespin
- adhesive tape
- wire strippers or a knife
- jug
- water
- teaspoon
- 2 lengths of thin insulated electrical wire, 20 in. long
- 1 length of thin insulated electrical wire, 3 ft. long

Preparation: Strip some wire

Page 19 shows how to strip wire. You'll need two pieces of wire about 20 inches long.

(a)

Wrap the stripped end of one of the wires tightly around the screw, just under the screw's head.

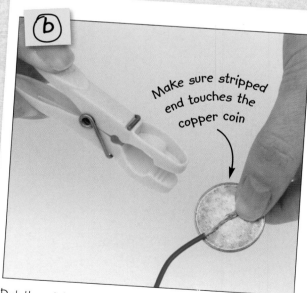

(b)

Make sure stripped end touches the copper coin

Put the stripped end of the second wire on top of the copper coin and hold it on using a clothespin.

See page 19 for how to make a current detector.

Twist together each of the remaining stripped ends of the two insulated wires to the ends of the current detector. Using adhesive tape, attach the current detector to your work surface (to stop it moving around later).

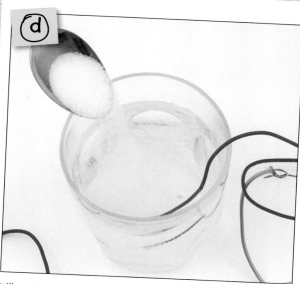

Fill a glass with water and stir in a couple of teaspoons of table salt. Put the screw underwater in the glass.

Carefully lower the coin into the water (don't let the coin touch the screw). As you do this, watch the needle on the current detector very closely. What happens? Take the pin out again – what happens?

Q Can coins and screws make electricity?

A Yes, by putting them in salty water.

The screw and the coin are made of two different metals (the screw is coated in zinc and the coin is copper). The water contains tiny particles with an electric charge. The different metals make the particles move through the water, and this makes an electric current – you should've seen the current detector twitch slightly as electricity was generated. Batteries work in a similar way.

21

MAGIC magnet

This experiment shows that electricity can be used to make a magnet that will pick up small metal objects. The magnet can be switched on and off.

15 min | Help needed | Tricky

You will need

- work surface
- large steel nail (or screw)
- thin insulated electrical wire, 3 ft.
- 1.5V AA battery
- sticky tack
- paper clips
- adhesive tape
- wire strippers or a knife
- short, thick elastic band

Preparation: Strip some wire

Page 19 shows how to strip wire. You'll need two pieces of wire about 3 feet long.

Preparation: Make an electromagnet

Put sticky tack on the nail first to help hold the wire in place

Starting about 4 inches from one end of the wire, wrap the wire tightly around the length of the nail up to the nail's head.

(a)

Put a small elastic band lengthways around the battery so that it goes over both metal terminals.

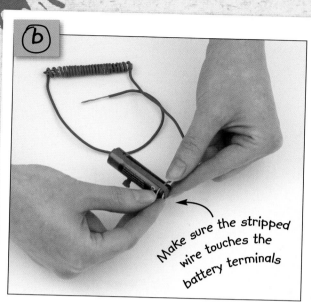

ⓑ

Make sure the stripped wire touches the battery terminals

Put each of the stripped ends of the wire from the electromagnet under the elastic band at each end of the battery.

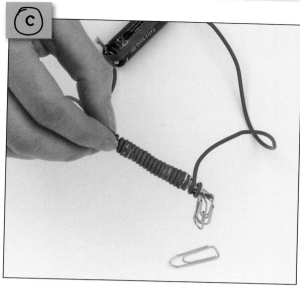

ⓒ

Put a few paper clips on the work surface. Hold the electromagnet with the pointy end of the nail close to the paper clips. Watch what happens to the paper clips. Don't leave the wire connected to the battery for more than a few seconds at a time, otherwise the battery will quickly run down and become hot.

ⓠ Can electricity pick up a paper clip?

ⓐ Yes, the electricity turns the nail or screw into an electromagnet. The electromagnet pulls on the paper clips because they are made of steel. When you take the wire away from the battery, the electricity stops flowing, so the electromagnet stops working and the paper clips fall back to the table.

ⓓ

After a few seconds, take one of the wires away from the battery. What happens to the paper clips now?

Also try...

Make an electromagnet using twice as much wire. Adding another battery in series with the first, use another piece of foil to connect the two batteries end to end (make sure both are the same way around). Adding more wire and more batteries should make the electromagnet stronger. Can you pick up more paper clips now?

Buzz!
BUZZ!

Using an electromagnet, you can create a noise by making and breaking a circuit. This experiment shows you how to build a buzzer.

30 min   Help needed   Hard

Preparation: Make a circuit

Page 14 shows how to make your basic circuit. You'll only need one piece of foil, and only follow stages a, b, and c.

You will need

- work surface
- medium-sized metal paper clip
- adhesive tape
- empty aluminum soda can
- scissors
- 1.5V AA battery
- short, thick elastic band
- one length of aluminum foil, 8 in. x 1 in.
- large steel nail
- thin insulated electrical wire, 3 ft.
- wire strippers or a knife

Preparation: Make an electromagnet

See page 22 for how to make an electromagnet.

a

Straighten out the first two bends of the paper clip, so you have a straight piece of wire with a hook at one end.

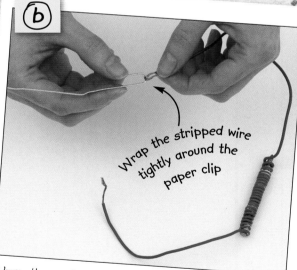

b

Wrap the stripped wire tightly around the paper clip

Wrap the end of one of the stripped wires from the electromagnet around the bend of the hook in the clip.

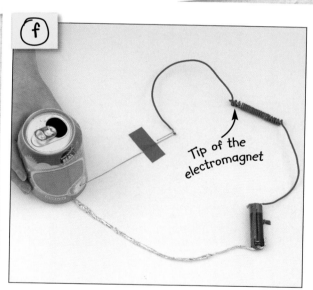

c

Tape the loop in the paper clip firmly to your work surface. Gently bend it upwards so that the straight end is about 1 inch above the work surface.

e

Ask an adult to scrape off the ink from one side of the can to make a patch of bare metal. Tape the spare end of the foil strip (attached to the battery) to the underside of the can.

d

Put the spare stripped end of the electromagnet under the elastic band at one end of the battery, touching the terminal.

f

Tip of the electromagnet

Stand the can next to the straightened paper clip so that the end just touches the bare metal patch on the can.

Q Can an electromagnet make noise?

A **Yes, by making a buzzer.** The parts of the buzzer make an electric circuit. The electricity flows from the battery, through the can, along the paper clip, through the electromagnet and back to the battery. When the electromagnet is moved closer to the paper clip, it pulls the tip of the clip away from the can. This breaks the circuit, which turns off the electromagnet. As electricity stops flowing, the paper clip springs back to touch the can and reconnects the circuit. This happens again and again, making a buzzing noise.

g

Move the pointy end of the electromagnet slowly towards the center of the straight part of the paper clip and listen carefully. What can you hear? If it doesn't work, adjust the distance between the electromagnet and the paper clip.

25

MAGIC moving wire

Some of the other experiments in this book showed how electricity can make magnets, and wires with electricity in them make magnets move. In this experiment, you can see how electricity and magnets can make a wire move.

30 min — Help needed — Hard

You will need

- work surface
- 1.5V AA battery
- 2 lengths of aluminum foil, 8 in. x 1 in.
- short, thick elastic band
- 3 lengths of copper wire, 2.5 in. x 4.5 in.
- bar magnet
- wire strippers, knife or pliers
- adhesive tape
- scissors

Preparation: Make a circuit

Page 14 shows how to make your basic circuit. You'll only need two pieces of foil, and only follow stages a, b, and c.

(a) Tape the two long pieces of copper wire to your work surface, parallel to each other, about 1.5 inches apart.

(b) Fold the foil around the copper wire

Take your circuit, and attach the ends of the foil strips to the copper wire.

(c)

Put the shorter piece of copper wire across the two longer wires, completing the electric circuit. Hold one end of the magnet just above the center of the shorter wire, and watch what happens. Don't leave the shorter wire in place for long as it will quickly make the battery run down.

Q Can a magnet move a copper wire?

A Yes, if a magnet is placed near a wire that has an electric current running through it. When electricity flows through the copper wire, it becomes a magnet itself. The bar magnet creates a magnetic field around the copper wire. This pushes the wire, so it rolls along. This is called the motor effect. All electric motors use this to work.

As the short piece of copper wire moves, the electric circuit stays intact

Also try...

Turn the magnet around so the opposite end is near the wire. The wire should move in the opposite direction from before because you are using the opposite pole of the magnet. Now try swapping the pieces of foil, so they touch opposite terminals on the battery. The wire should move the opposite way, too, because the electricity flows in the opposite direction through the wire.

Electricity with SALT

Some liquids let electricity flow through them. In this experiment you can see how electricity flows through salty water.

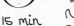

15 min   No help needed   Tricky

Preparation: Make a circuit

Page 14 shows how to make your basic circuit. You'll only need one piece of foil, and only follow stages a, b, and c.

Preparation: Make a current detector

Page 19 shows how to make a current detector.

You will need

- work surface
- glass
- 1.5V AA battery
- short, thick elastic band
- table salt
- thin insulated electrical wire, 3 ft.
- 2 lengths of aluminum foil, 8 in. x 1 in.
- adhesive tape
- wire strippers or a knife
- scissors
- compass
- water

(a)

Put one of the stripped wire ends from the current detector under the elastic band at one end of the battery (attached to the foil strip on the circuit).

28

b) Fill the glass with water. Fold the spare end of the foil (attached to the battery) over the lip of the glass, so that the last couple inches are in the water. In the same way, fold a spare strip of foil over the lip of the glass.

d) Add a teaspoon of salt to the water in the jar and gently stir it in. Repeat step c again. What happens this time?

c) Attach the second strip of foil to the spare stripped end of the electricity detector. What happens to the compass needle?

Q) Can salt make electricity flow?

A) **Yes, when you add salt to the water, more electricity flows.** The compass needle in the current detector twitches if the wire touches the foil, because the circuit is complete. With plain water in the jar, only a tiny amount of electricity flows. When you add salt, the amount of electricity increases, so the needle twitches more. This happens because the salt breaks into tiny particles that are charged with electricity, which then carries the electricity through the water.

Quiz ZONE

Get ready to test how much you've learned from the experiments in this book. Write down your answers on a piece of paper and then check them against the answers on page 31. No cheating!

Q2 picture clue

What is the missing word?

① A balloon picks up paper when it is charged with _____ electricity.

② By connecting a bulb to a battery with a conductor, you make a loop called a _____ .

③ The flow of electricity around a circuit is called an _____ .

④ A _____ battery terminal is marked with a + symbol.

⑤ A _____ battery terminal is marked with a - symbol.

Q8 picture clue

What word beginning with...

⑥ B gives the "push" for electricity to flow around a circuit?

⑦ I is the name for materials that don't conduct electricity?

⑧ D helps us to identify if electricity is flowing along a wire?

⑨ R happens when two objects with the same charge are pushed together?

True or false?

10 Two positive charges will attract each other.

11 Some photocopiers use static electricity to work.

12 If you rub your hair with a balloon, your hair will stand on end.

Q12 picture clue

Multiple choice

13 If electricity is sent through two lightbulbs at the same time, are they parallel, twin, or aligned?

14 Are metals conductors, insulators, or transmitters?

15 Can nails and coins make electricity by being put in fresh water, salty water, or hot water?

16 If two lightbulbs are in a "series" circuit, will the light be off, dim, or bright?

Q15 picture clue

Q20 picture clue

Remember, remember

17 Can you get rid of static electricity?

18 Will electricity flow through plastic?

19 Does water conduct electricity?

20 Can a magnet move a copper wire?

31

quiz answers

1. Static 2. Circuit 3. Electric current 4. Positive 5. Negative
6. Battery 7. Insulator 8. Detector 9. Repel 10. False
11. True 12. True 13. Parallel 14. Conductors 15. Salty water
16. Dim 17. Yes 18. No 19. Yes 20. Yes, if a magnet is placed near a wire that has an electric current running through it.

GLOSSARY

Attract To draw two objects with opposite charges together (opposite of repel).

Charge A property that causes particles to attract or repel each other. Objects can have either a positive or negative charge.

Circuit A loop through which electricity can flow.

Conductor A material, such as copper, which allows the flow of an electrical current.

Detector A device that recognizes the presence of electricity in a circuit.

Electromagnet A strong magnet that is only magnetic when an electric current passes through it.

Insulator A material, such as rubber, that does not conduct electricity.

Magnetic field The area around a magnet inside which its magnetic force can be detected. An electric current creates a magnetic field.

Negative charge When a substance is negatively charged, it gains electrons.

Parallel circuit A circuit where an equal amount of electricity flows through two objects, such as lightbulbs, at the same time.

Positive charge When a substance becomes positively charged, it loses electrons.

Repel To push two objects with the same charge away from each other (opposite of attract).

Series circuit A circuit where electricity flows through one object, such as a lightbulb, and then on to another object.

Terminal The ends of a battery. One is positive and one is negative.

INDEX

WEBSITES

Due to the changing nature of Internet links, PowerKids Press has developed an online list of websites related to the subject of this book. This site is updated regularly. Please use this link to access the list:
www.powerkidslinks.com/ese/elecmag